Prayers and Decrees for the Soul of the Woman

Healing from What She Doesn't Speak About

Ashlyn Meraz

Dedication

I dedicate this book to the women who have felt silenced in their pain, who carried the weight of life's struggles alone, and who questioned if freedom was ever truly possible.

To the woman still fighting to find her voice.

To the woman standing up for the little girl within her, the one no one ever stood up for.

To the woman healing from the things she's never said out loud.

This is for you. You are seen, you are heard, and you are not alone.

Table of Contents

Introduction

Hello There,

First and foremost, I want to say how excited I am for what's about to take place in your life as you read this book. *Prayers and Decrees for the Soul* was birthed from my personal journey—one of healing, breaking generational curses, and stepping into my God-given identity. Through the love of Christ and an intimate relationship with the Father, Son, and Holy Spirit, I've overcome many of the very struggles written in these pages and I continue to walk through healing in others.

Throughout this journey, I've come to understand the undeniable power of praying, declaring, and decreeing God's Word over my life. My prayer is that as you speak the words within this book, the love of Christ will break every stronghold and dismantle every form of bondage that has kept you in cycles God never intended for you to live in.

There is one thing required of you as you embark on this journey...
FAITH.
You must believe wholeheartedly, that your Heavenly Father is backing every declaration you release.

Each page is designed to break, dismantle, cancel, and bind every negative word spoken over your life and every thought pattern, tradition, and habit that contradicts who God says you are. But it doesn't stop there. These pages are also designed to *loose, build, encourage*, and *equip* you to stir your spirit and help you move through life with boldness, knowing that the things meant to break you have already been defeated.

So with that being said...

Let's break the chains and walk boldly into freedom.
Now.. what does it mean to declare and decree?

Preface

Maybe you've heard the words *declare* and *decree* before but never truly understood what they mean and that's completely okay. That's why I feel it's so important to pause and clearly explain what I'm encouraging you to speak over your life.

In the spiritual realm, the words we speak carry power. Scripture tells us that "life and death are in the power of the tongue" (Proverbs 18:21), which means our words have the ability to shape atmospheres, shift mindsets, and unlock breakthroughs. But before we begin to speak with authority, it's important to understand what it actually means to **declare** and **decree** — and why both are vital tools for the believer.

Prologue

What is a Declaration?

A *declaration* is a bold confession of faith. It is when you *speak aloud* what God has said in His Word or what you believe to be true in agreement with His promises. When you declare something, you are aligning your words with heaven, speaking forth what already exists in the spiritual realm even if you don't see it yet in the natural.

To declare is to *announce*, *affirm*, or *proclaim* something as truth , especially when it's tied to a promise of God.

Examples of declarations:

- "I am fearfully and wonderfully made." (Psalm 139:14)

- "I walk in divine favor."

- "I am the head and not the tail, above and not beneath." (Deuteronomy 28:13)

Declarations build faith, shift your mindset, and remind your soul of who God is and what He's promised.

What is a Decree?

A *decree* is a legal term. In the natural, a decree is an official order issued by someone in authority — like a king, judge, or governing body that must be carried out. Spiritually, when you decree, you are *legislating from a place of authority in Christ*, commanding God's will to be established on earth as it is in heaven.

To decree is to issue a command, backed by heaven's authority. You're not just speaking hope, you're activating spiritual law and enforcing Kingdom order. Examples of decrees:

- "I decree that every generational curse is broken off my bloodline in Jesus' name."

- "I decree divine healing over my body."

- "I decree that doors of provision and opportunity are opening now."

Decrees go beyond affirmations, they *enforce* what's already been written in the courts of heaven. **Job 22:28** says, *"You will also decree a thing, and it will be established for you."*

Why is it Important to Declare and Decree?

Because your words carry power.

As believers, we're not just speaking into the air — we're speaking with authority and partnering with Heaven. When you declare and decree, you're not simply hoping for change , you're **activating** it. You are aligning your mouth with God's Word, and that alignment has the power to shift atmospheres, break chains, and call things forth that have not yet manifested in the natural.

Declaring and decreeing is how you remind your soul of what God has said, silence the lies of the enemy, and boldly speak what must come into alignment with Heaven. It's not just about positive affirmations — it's **spiritual enforcement**. You're not begging for breakthrough, you're standing in your **God-given authority**, boldly declaring: *"This is what God said — and it shall be so."*

Your words matter.

"Death and life are in the power of the tongue, and those who love it will eat its fruit."
— Proverbs 18:21

"You will also decree a thing, and it will be established for you; and light will shine on your ways."
— Job 22:28

Speak life. Speak truth. Speak with boldness.

Heaven is backing YOU.

SECTION 1

Identity & Inner Healing

Chapter 1:

When You're Wrestling with Worth

For the Woman Who Thinks/Believes "I Am Not Enough"

"Thank you for making me so wonderfully complex! Your workmanship is marvelous—how well I know it". -Psalm 139:14

Prayer

Heavenly Father, I confess that I've believed the lie that I am not enough. But today, I lay down every label, insecurity, and word curse that has made me feel inadequate. I receive Your truth, that I am created in Your image, beautifully and wonderfully made, chosen by You, and made whole in Christ. Let every hidden place be filled with Your identity, your truth and every false belief be uprooted and replaced with divine confidence. In Jesus' name, Amen.

I Declare and Decree

I declare that I am fearfully and wonderfully made (Psalm 139:14), chosen, loved, and seen by God; who I am is defined solely by Him, complete in Christ and lacking nothing (Colossians 2:10), and I decree that every lie of inadequacy and insecurity is broken off my life, my voice, presence, and purpose carry weight in the Kingdom, and I will rise in holy confidence, clothed in the righteousness of Christ, walking boldly in rooms I once felt unworthy of.

For the Woman Who Thinks God Does Not Love Her

"And I am convinced that nothing can ever separate us from God's love. Neither death nor life, neither angels nor demons, neither our fears for today nor our worries about tomorrow—not even the powers of hell can separate us from God's love. No power in the sky above or in the earth below—indeed, nothing in all creation will ever be able to separate us from the love of God that is revealed in Christ Jesus our Lord."-Romans 8:38-39

Prayer

Lord, there are moments where I feel unlovable , some days I feel like Your love couldn't possibly include someone like me. But I silence the lies that distort Your heart. Your Word says nothing can separate me from Your love. So Today, I receive that truth. Help me to feel it, believe it, and live from it. Wrap me in Your presence and remind me that I am deeply, endlessly loved and cherished. In Jesus' name, Amen.

I Declare and Decree

I declare that I am loved by God with an everlasting love (Jeremiah 31:3), not abandoned but held, the beloved daughter of the Most High King, worthy of God's love not because of what I've done but because of who He is; and I decree that every lie of rejection and abandonment is broken now, the love of God floods every void in my heart, and I will walk in the fullness of God's love without fear or shame.

For the Woman Who Thinks "I'm Not Qualified"

"It is not that we think we are qualified to do anything on our own. Our qualification comes from God. He has enabled us to be ministers of his new covenant. This is a covenant not of written laws, but of the Spirit. The old written covenant ends in death; but under the new covenant, the Spirit gives life." -2 Corinthians 3:5-6

Prayer

Heavenly Father, I've let fear and self-doubt convince me that I'm not qualified for the very things You've called me to. Thoughts of self-doubt creep in and make me question my skills , talents and gifts. But Your grace is what makes me able. You don't wait until I have it all together , You use me right in the middle of the process. Remind me that my qualification comes from You, not my past or my résumé. I surrender every excuse and step into purpose by faith. In Jesus' name, Amen.

I Declare and Decree

I declare that I am equipped and empowered by God, called, anointed, and sent, not defined by my past but aligned with my purpose, and qualified through Christ who strengthens me (Philippians 4:13); and I decree that I will no longer shrink back from divine assignments, that fear, imposter syndrome, and insecurity have no place in my life, that the doors God opens for me, no one can shut (Revelation 3:8), and that I will walk in supernatural boldness and divine clarity.

For the Woman Struggling to Love Herself

(Eyes, Ears, Nose, Teeth, Lips, and All That Makes Her Unique)

"You are altogether beautiful, my darling, beautiful in every way." -Song of Songs 4:7

Prayer

Heavenly Father,

I come before You with the parts of myself I've silently criticized and rejected, the features You crafted by hand. I've looked in the mirror and struggled to love what I see. I've compared, hidden, and even wished I looked like someone else. But You, Lord, make no mistakes. Your Word says I am fearfully and wonderfully made — every part of me, even the ones I've questioned and hated, are marked with Your intention. I ask that you heal my wounds of comparison. Silence the voices that told me I wasn't beautiful. Help me to see myself through Your eyes with honor, love, and awe. Teach me to embrace my reflection, not with pride, but with gratitude. Let my confidence be rooted in who You are and how You formed me. In Jesus' name, Amen.

I Declare and Decree

I declare that I am made in the image of God, perfectly and intentionally designed (Genesis 1:27), not a mistake, with every feature carrying His fingerprint; I am beautiful, valuable, and worthy inside and out, learning to love what God lovingly created, and not defined by society's standards but by Heaven's design; and I decree that the spirit of self-hate and insecurity is broken off my life, that I will no longer reject the parts of me God has called beautiful, that I will walk in holy confidence embracing the uniqueness of my features, that I am radiant with beauty, fearfully and wonderfully made in every detail, and that the mirror is no longer my enemy but a reminder of my divine identity.

Breaking Emotional Strongholds

For the Woman Struggling with Emotional Strongholds

(Anger, Resentment, Rejection, Unforgiveness, Bitterness, Shame, Unworthiness,Fear)

"We use God's mighty weapons, not worldly weapons, to knock down the strongholds of human reasoning and to destroy false arguments. We destroy every proud obstacle that keeps people from knowing God. We capture their rebellious thoughts and teach them to obey Christ."

-2 Corinthians 10:4-5

Prayer

Abba, I bring You the heaviness I've carried far too long. All of the anger, the resentment, the unforgiveness, the guilt, the depression, fear and the quiet torment of not feeling good enough. These emotional strongholds have taken up space in my heart, mind, body and in my soul. Today, I invite You into those spaces. Tear down every wall I've built to protect myself. Shine Your light in the dark corners of my soul. I surrender the pain, hurt and betrayal and pick up Your peace. Heal me deeply. Deliver me fully. And remind me that I am not what I feel. I am who You say I am. In Jesus' name, Amen.

I Declare and Decree

I declare that I am not my emotions—I am God's daughter; forgiven, redeemed, and set free from the weight of anger, resentment, rejection, unforgiveness, bitterness, shame, unworthiness, and fear; no longer bitter but better through Christ; worthy of love, joy, peace, and healing; emotionally whole and spiritually grounded in God's truth; and I decree that every emotional stronghold in my heart, mind, and soul is broken by the blood of Jesus, that bitterness and resentment have no place in my heart, that shame is replaced by divine acceptance, that depression is lifting off my life and joy is returning, and that I walk in emotional freedom, wholeness, and inner peace.

For the Woman Refusing to Ask for Help

"Share each other's burdens, and in this way obey the law of Christ."
-Galatians 6:2

Prayer

God, I confess that I've made strength my shield and silence my survival. I've learned to suffer quietly, thinking it's noble not to ask for help. But You didn't create me to carry everything alone. Your Word says Your strength is made perfect in my weakness. So today Heavenly Father, I lay down pride, fear, and the need to have it all together. Teach me how to lean on You, Teach me how to accept the help of others and allow them in with holy discernment. I don't want to just survive. I don't want to do life alone. I want to heal. In Jesus' name, Amen.

I Declare and Decree

I declare that I am not weak for needing help but very wise for asking; not a burden and worthy of support; surrounded by people God has assigned to walk with me; letting go of isolation and choosing connection; learning to receive help without guilt or shame; and I decree that pride and fear are being uprooted from my life, that I will no longer suffer in silence, that divine connections and safe spaces are coming into my life, that my healing journey will be walked with people who truly love and support me, and that vulnerability is my strength, not my weakness.

For the Woman Who Struggles with the Idea of Not Having to Be Strong Enough

"Each time he said, 'My grace is all you need. My power works best in weakness.' So now I am glad to boast about my weaknesses, so that the power of Christ can work through me." -2 Corinthians 12:9

Prayer

Lord, I've worn strength like armor because I didn't know any other way. But behind the strength is a tired heart and a weary body. I deeply desire rest, safety, and softness. I've believed the lie that I always have to be the strong one. But You're teaching me that true strength is found in surrender. Lord, Help me to lay it all down at your feet. The pressure, the performance, the "I got it." Teach me that You are my strength. It's okay to rest. It's okay to breathe. It's okay to be held. In Jesus' name, Amen.

I Declare and Decree

I declare that I am strong, yet I don't have to carry everything alone; safe to rest in God's arms; enough even when I'm not doing it all; allowed to feel, to be, and to breathe without guilt; learning to rest in God's strength, not rely on my own; and I decree that the pressure to be the strong one is breaking off of mc, that I am free from performance and people-pleasing, and that rest, safety, softness, and stillness are my holy portion.

For the Woman Struggling with Suicidal Thoughts

"I will not die; instead, I will live to tell what the Lord has done."

-Psalm 118:17

Prayer

Father,

Right now, I bring before You the thoughts that I've been too afraid to say out loud. The weight feels unbearable and the burden is heavy. The lies scream louder than truth. But even in the darkness, I know You see me. Your word affirms that you are the God who rescues, who redeems, and who revives.

Lord, I confess that I've believed the lie that I'd be better off gone , that my life doesn't matter, that I'm too broken to be healed and that no one loves me. But today, I choose to fight for my life. I may feel weak, but Your strength is holding me up. Breathe life back into my lungs. Patch up my wounded heart and renew my mind . Remind me that I have purpose, even when I feel like I don't. Surround me with people who will speak life over me. Cover me with Your peace and silence every tormenting voice of the enemy. In Jesus' name, Amen

I Declare and Decree

I declare that I am not alone because God is near to the brokenhearted (Psalm 34:18); not forgotten as Heaven knows my name and counts every tear; not a mistake but divinely created with purpose; not defined by my feelings but by who God says I am; loved, needed, still here, and that my life matters; and I decree that the spirit of suicide is broken off my life by the blood of Jesus, that I shall live and not die and declare the works of the Lord (Psalm 118:17), that every tormenting voice of darkness in my life is silenced by God's truth, that hope is being restored to my heart right now, that purpose, healing, and peace are rising in me even now, and that this is not the end of my story but the beginning of a new chapter.

Chapter 3:

Healing From the Past

For the Woman Called to Break Generational Curses

"You must not bow down to them or worship them, for I, the Lord your God, am a jealous God who will not tolerate your affection for any other gods. I lay the sins of the parents upon their children; the entire family is affected—even children in the third and fourth generations of those who reject me. But I lavish unfailing love for a thousand generations on those who love me and obey my commands. -Exodus 20:5-6

Prayer

Heavenly Father,

I recognize that I've been carrying burdens that didn't start with me. Patterns of pain, dysfunction, addictions, behaviors, fears and silence have followed my family for generations. But today, I choose to be the one who breaks the cycle. By the authority of Jesus Christ, I renounce every curse, every stronghold, and every generational pattern that is not aligned with Your Word. Heal the bloodline through me, Lord. I have faith and trust that you can do it. Let what starts with me shift everything that comes after me. In Jesus' name, Amen.

I Decree and Decree

I declare that I am the curse-breaker in my family, covered by the blood of Jesus and walking in covenant, not curses; I am the new pattern, the change agent, and the shifter in my lineage; no longer bound by what happened before me, and anointed to build what others never had the strength to finish; I decree that generational curses are broken off of me and my lineage, that I am the first of many to walk in total freedom, that cycles of trauma, addiction, and silence end with me, and that my bloodline is covered and redeemed through Jesus Christ; a new legacy of healing, faith, and purpose begins now.

For the Woman Healing from Childhood Trauma

(Including abuse, neglect, fear, or abandonment)

"The Spirit of the Sovereign Lord is upon me, for the Lord has anointed me to bring good news to the poor. He has sent me to comfort the brokenhearted and to proclaim that captives will be released and prisoners will be freed."- Isaiah 61:1

Prayer

Lord,
There are wounds from my childhood that still affect the way I see You, others, and myself. Some of the pain I endured, I've never even spoken out loud because of fear and shame. But You saw it all. You were there. I give You the parts of my past that still hurt , the memories, the silence, the confusion, the betrayal. Heal the little girl in me who never felt safe. Restore the parts of me that were stolen before I even understood what was happening. Hold me in the places where I still feel small. Rewrite my story with Your love. In Jesus' name, Amen.

I Declare and Decree

I declare that I am not what happened to me, but who God is healing me to become; I am safe now, seen, known, and nurtured by my Heavenly Father; healing layer by layer, day by day; not defined by my past, but delivered by His love. I decree that childhood trauma no longer holds power over my identity; that the emotional residue of my past is being washed away; that every place where I was broken is being restored with wholeness; that the child within me is being healed, loved, and protected; and that I walk in freedom from trauma—mind, body, and spirit.

For the Woman Healing from Abuse & Molestation

(Sexual, physical, or emotional trauma)

"He heals the brokenhearted and bandages their wounds."-Psalm 147:3

Prayer

Jesus,
What was done to me was not my fault , but it wounded me deeply. I've wrestled with shame, confusion, anger, and silence. There are parts of me I've tried to hide, memories I've tried to forget, and moments I still can't make sense of. I feel broken, But today, I bring it all to You. You are the Healer of deep wounds and the Defender of the broken. Wash me in Your love. Break every soul tie, every traumatic imprint, and every lie attached to the abuse. Restore what was violated in me . I want to reclaim my body, my mind, and my worth in you lord . In Jesus' name, Amen.

I Declare and Decree

I declare that I am not what happened to me, but made new in Christ; I am not dirty, but pure, whole, and cleansed by the blood of Jesus; I am not to blame for what happened to me, and the shame is not mine to carry; I am worthy of love, safety, and healing; and I am free from the hold of past abuse. I decree that every soul tie and traumatic imprint is broken in Jesus' name; that the spirit of shame, fear, and guilt is cast out of my life; that my body and mind are being restored in truth and peace; that I am not a victim, but victorious in the mighty name of Jesus; and that my story is not over, for God is rewriting it for His glory and using it as my divine testimony to help others.

For the Woman Healing from Parental Wounds

(From absence, rejection, control, abandonment, neglect, emotional or spiritual abuse)

"Even if my father and mother abandon me, the Lord will hold me close." -Psalm 27:10

Prayer

Heavenly Father,

You know the pain I've carried up until now. The ache that comes from being wounded by the very people who were supposed to love, protect, and guide me, harsh words or unmet needs. I've been left with scars that still bleed. I confess that I've carried resentment, disappointment, and even guilt towards (Say which parent or if it's both say both names) , I've spent my life trying to fill the void they left behind. But today, I surrender that pain to You. I no longer want to carry what's not mine to hold. Heal the parts of me that were shaped by rejection, control, abandonment, or unmet love. Re-father me, Lord. Re-mother me. Teach me what love, affirmation, safety, and correction look like through *You*. Help me to forgive, not for their sake, but for mine , so I can walk free in my salvation . In Jesus' name, Amen.

I Declare and Decree

I declare I am no longer bound by parental wounds and choose to forgive, knowing I am a beloved daughter of God. I am filled with His presence, loved, and whole. I decree that pain, bitterness, and emotional wounds are being healed and uprooted. I am no longer defined by absence but by God's faithfulness. I am free to love, forgive, and break generational cycles.

SECTION 2

Healing the Heart & Mind

Chapter 4:

Trauma, Grief, and Loss

For the Woman Struggling with the Loss of a Parent or Grandparent

"God blesses those who mourn, for they will be comforted."-Matthew 5:4

Prayer

Lord,

The pain of losing a parent is one I never imagined I'd carry. Whether it was sudden or slow, expected or unfair — their absence has left a gap nothing else seems to fill. I miss their voice. I miss their presence. I miss what could've been. I bring You my grief, my unanswered questions, and my quiet tears. Comfort me, Lord. Wrap me in the peace that surpasses understanding. Help me honor their memory, but not be paralyzed by their absence. Give me grace for the days that still hurt. In Jesus' name, Amen.

I Declare and Decree

I declare that I can grieve and trust in God's comfort. I am growing in hope and healing, never alone because God is by my side. I decree that grief won't consume me, peace replaces my sorrow, my heart heals with every step, I honor their memory without regret, and joy can shine even through loss.

For the Woman Struggling with the Loss of a Partner

"The Lord is close to the brokenhearted; he rescues those whose spirits are crushed."-Psalm 34:18

Prayer

Heavenly Father ,

The loss of someone I loved deeply has left me broken in ways I can't explain. Whether it was through death, betrayal, or separation , the ache is real, and the silence is loud. I bring You my shattered heart, my memories, and the unanswered questions. Hold me through the nights I cry and speak peace over the days I feel numb. Teach me that love doesn't die — it transforms. Help me grieve with hope and heal with grace. Let this be the beginning of a new chapter, not the end of my story. In Jesus' name, Amen.

I Declare and Decree

I declare that loss does not define me because God is holding me through every moment. Even in my deepest sorrow, I am strong. I give myself permission to mourn what I've lost while still believing that something beautiful can rise from the pain. God's love carries me through every wave of grief, and little by little, my heart is healing. I decree that my broken heart is being made whole again. I will not stay stuck in the hurt from the past. New joy, new strength, and a clear purpose are growing inside me. I choose to let go of guilt, blame, and the things I couldn't control. Love—starting with God's perfect love—will find me again and bring new life to my soul.

For the Woman Struggling with the Loss of a Child

"I will comfort you there in Jerusalem as a mother comforts her child."

-Isaiah 66:13

Prayer

Jesus,
There are no words for this kind of pain , the pain of losing a piece of me. Whether it was through miscarriage, stillbirth, illness, or tragedy, I am grieving the life of a child who changed me forever. Lord, only You can comfort a heart this broken. Be near to me. Carry me through the waves. Wrap me in Your presence. Remind me that You hold my baby in Your arms — and You are holding me too. Turn my sorrow into strength. Help me to live, even when I feel like a part of me died. In Jesus' name, Amen.

I Declare and Decree

I declare that I am a mother, even as I grieve. I give myself permission to mourn while still trusting in God's goodness. I am comforted by the God who understands what it means to lose a Son. His love carries me through every tear and every memory. I am not alone in this pain, God weeps with me. I decree that my womb, my heart, and my spirit are healing. I will not live in guilt, fear, or shame, but in God's peace. The spirit of grief will not consume me. Joy will come back into my life, even if it comes slowly. My child's life has meaning, and so does mine.

For the Woman Struggling with the Loss of a Relative

(Aunt, Uncle, Grandparent, Cousin, Sibling, or Someone Deeply Loved)

"He will wipe every tear from their eyes, and there will be no more death or sorrow or crying or pain. All these things are gone forever."

-Revelation 21:4

Prayer

Lord,
Losing someone I loved , someone who held a special place in my life , Lord it has left me feeling a deep ache. Whether they were a constant presence or someone I wish I had more time with, their absence is real, and the grief comes in waves. I miss the sound of their voice, their laughter, the way they made me feel seen and known. I bring You my sadness, my questions, and even my anger. Help me process this loss without guilt or shame. Teach me how to grieve well, to feel without becoming consumed, and to honor their memory while still moving forward. Remind me that mourning is not weakness — it's love in its purest form. Wrap me in comfort.

Let my heart begin to heal, piece by piece. In Jesus' name, Amen.

I Declare and Decree

I declare that it's okay for me to grieve without feeling judged. I feel comfort from the Holy Spirit. I'm learning to remember the good times while healing from the loss. God's love surrounds me in every sad moment. I'm not alone—God is with me on this journey. I decree that peace will protect my heart and mind even when I'm hurting (Philippians 4:7). My sadness won't control me, and healing is coming. I can think of them with love, not just pain. God gives me strength every day. My heart will heal, and happiness will come back.

Chapter 5:

Shame, Guilt, and Forgiveness

For the Woman Struggling to Forgive

(Whether it's a betrayal, offense, or wound that changed everything)

"Make allowance for each other's faults, and forgive anyone who offends you. Remember, the Lord forgave you, so you must forgive others."-Colossians 3:13

Prayer

Lord,

You know the depth of the pain I've experienced — and You know how hard it's been to forgive. I've carried the weight of what they did and how it made me feel. The bitterness has settled in places that You never meant for me to carry. But today, I choose to surrender the offense, not because they deserve it, but because *I* deserve peace. Teach me what real forgiveness looks like. Help me release the debt they owe me into Your hands and trust that You are the God of justice. Let forgiveness set me free. In Jesus' name, Amen.

I Declare and Decree

I declare that I'm not stuck in bitterness. I'm choosing to live free. I have the strength to forgive because Christ lives in me. I'm letting go of the pain instead of replaying it. I'd rather walk in grace than hold a grudge. I'm choosing peace over staying offended.

I decree that unforgiveness is losing its power in my life. I don't have to carry the weight of what someone else did. Forgiveness is helping me heal. I'm no longer tied to the pain—I'm connected to the One who heals. I'm moving forward without resentment, and I'm finally free.

For the Woman Struggling to Forgive Herself for Abortions

"But if we confess our sins to him, he is faithful and just to forgive us our sins and to cleanse us from all wickedness."-1 John 1:9

Prayer

God,

You know the secret I've carried — the pain, the shame, the guilt that I've tucked away. I've replayed my decision over and over again, wondering if You could ever forgive me. But today, I lay my burden down at Your feet. I ask You to wash me, redeem me, and heal the part of me that still grieves. I choose to believe that Your grace is bigger than my past, and Your blood covers even this. I release the shame. I forgive myself. I receive Your mercy and choose to walk in freedom. In Jesus' name, Amen.

I Declare and Decree

I declare that I am fully forgiven by God's grace. My past doesn't define me, His love does. I still deserve love, healing, and peace. I don't have to hide anymore—I'm healing. I'm not doing this alone., God is with me every step of the way. I decree that shame and guilt are no longer part of who I am. Every lie that says I'm not worthy is broken in Jesus' name. There's no condemnation for me because I belong to Christ (Romans 8:1). I'm walking in healing and purpose. My story will be a testimony, not something to be ashamed of.

For the Woman Struggling with Divorce

"But forget all that, it is nothing compared to what I am going to do. For I am about to do something new. See, I have already begun! Do you not see it? I will make a pathway through the wilderness. I will create rivers in the dry wasteland."-Isaiah 43:18-19

Prayer

Heavenly Father,

I never thought this would be my story. The pain of separation, the ache of disappointment, and the shame of starting over weigh heavy on my heart. I bring You the brokenness — the dreams that died, the vows that were shattered, and the wounds that still bleed. I ask for Your healing, Your strength, and Your peace. Restore my identity. Rebuild my confidence. Teach me that this ending is not the end of me. You are the God who restores and makes all things new. In Jesus' name, Amen.

I Declare and Decree

I declare that I am not defined by my divorce, I am still chosen, loved, and called by God. I'm healing, even if the process is messy. I am still worthy of love, restoration, and a new beginning. I am not disqualified—God is giving me a new definition through His grace. I am whole, even with a broken past. I decree that shame from divorce will not hold me back. God is rewriting my story with beauty, not bitterness. Every lie that says I have failed is being replaced with truth of I have survived. I'm moving forward, covered in grace and wisdom. God is healing every scar and restoring my joy.

SECTION 3

Discipline, Purity & Trusting God

Chapter 6:

When Control Gets in the Way

For the Woman Struggling with Control

"Trust in the Lord with all your heart; do not depend on your own understanding. Seek his will in all you do, and he will show you which path to take."-Proverbs 3:5-6

Prayer

Heavenly Father,

I confess that I've tried to take the lead in areas where You were supposed to go first. I've been driven by fear, by past letdowns, and by a need to protect myself. Holding onto control made me feel secure — but in reality, it's worn me down. I've exhausted myself trying to manage what only You can handle. Lord, help me to release the weight. Teach me to trust You again. I surrender the need to know every outcome, and I invite You to be the one who leads. You are faithful, and I can rest in that. In Jesus' name, Amen.

I Declare and Decree

I declare that I'm no longer a prisoner to control, I can live freely in Christ. I'm letting go and allowing God to be God. I'm learning to trust the unknown because I trust the One who knows everything. I don't have to be in charge of it all, and that brings me peace. I'm led by faith, not by fear. I decree that the spirit of fear and control is broken off my life. God's perfect will is unfolding, even when I can't see it. I trust in the Lord with all my heart and won't lean on my own understanding (Proverbs 3:5). I no longer try to control the outcome—I choose to wait in peace. My life is under God's order, and I walk in surrender.

For the Woman Who Struggles with Submitting

"So humble yourselves before God. Resist the devil, and he will flee from you." -James 4:7

Prayer

Lord,

I admit it, submission is something I've wrestled with. Not because I don't love You, but because I've feared what letting go might cost me. I've equated submission with losing myself or being taken advantage of. But You're showing me that submission is not about control, it's about trust. It's not about silence ,it's about surrender.

So today, I lay down my resistance. Teach me how to submit to You first, then to those You've divinely positioned in my life. Help me see submission as strength, not weakness — as protection, not punishment. Break down the walls that pride and pain have built. I choose to yield to Your will, even when it's uncomfortable. In Jesus' name, Amen.

I Declare and Decree

I declare that I am strong when I surrender. I am safe under God's authority. Humility empowers me, and obedience protects me. I am free from rebellion, pride, and fear of submission. I am aligned with God's divine order for my life.I decree that resistance and rebellion no longer rule my heart. I am submitted to God's will, timing, and process. Pride is being replaced with wisdom and grace. I choose to honor the roles and authority God has placed in my life. Submission is opening doors, protecting my purpose, and positioning me for blessings.

For the Woman Struggling to Trust

"You will keep in perfect peace all who trust in you, all whose thoughts are fixed on you!"-Isaiah 26:3

Prayer

Heavenly Father,

I want to trust , but if I'm honest, it's hard. I've been let down, lied to, disappointed, and wounded by the very people I tried to trust. And if I'm being even more honest, there are moments I've doubted You too. I've questioned Your timing, Your silence, and even Your protection. But today, I bring all my fears, all my doubt, and all my broken expectations to You. Heal my heart from the roots of distrust. Show me that trusting You is not a risk — it's the safest place I could ever be. Teach me how to trust again, one step at a time. In Jesus' name, Amen.

I Declare and Decree

I declare that I am learning to trust again—not blindly, but with wisdom. I feel safe when I place my trust in God. I'm healing from the things that made me guarded. I'm growing in discernment, not fear. I'm open to love, connection, and new beginnings as God leads me.I decree that fear, doubt, and distrust are breaking off of my heart. I won't let past pain affect future promises. God is rebuilding my trust—in Him, in others, and in myself. I no longer need control to feel safe; I have peace through Christ. I walk in wisdom, faith, and full confidence in God's plan.

Chapter 7:

Trusting God With Your Journey

For the Woman Wrestling With the Unknown, Desires of the Flesh, and Delays That Hurt

For the Woman Who is Anxious and Uncertain About Her Future

"For I know the plans I have for you," says the Lord. "They are plans for good and not for disaster, to give you a future and a hope."

- Jeremiah 29:11

Prayer

Heavenly Father,

There are so many questions in my heart — so many things I don't understand about where I'm going and what comes next. Anxiety has crept in, whispering doubt and fear. But I know You hold my future, even when I can't see the full picture. I surrender every worry, every timeline, every "what if" to You. Give me peace in the waiting and faith for the unknown. Help me to trust that You are writing a story far greater than I could imagine. In Jesus' name, Amen.

I Declare and Decree

I declare that I am not my fear—I am God's daughter, and He is faithful. I'm held in the hands of the One who already sees tomorrow. I'm choosing peace over anxiety and worship over worry. I'm not behind, I'm being prepared. I trust that I'm aligned with God's perfect timing.I decree that anxiety and fear about the future are breaking off of my life. I believe God's plans for me are full of hope and purpose (Jeremiah 29:11). I walk in peace, even without all the answers. I won't rush ahead of God—I will wait in faith.

For the Woman Struggling with Abstinence

"Don't you realize that your body is the temple of the Holy Spirit, who lives in you and was given to you by God? You do not belong to yourself, for God bought you with a high price. So you must honor God with your body."- 1 Corinthians 6:19-20

Prayer

Lord,
You know the war between my spirit and my flesh. You know how hard it is to stay committed to purity when desire, loneliness, and temptation creep in. I want to honor You with my body, but some days I feel weak. Strengthen me. Remind me that my body is a temple and that discipline is a form of worship. Help me not to settle for temporary pleasure that leads to spiritual emptiness. Guard my heart, my mind, and my emotions. In Jesus' name, Amen.

I Declare and Decree

I declare that I am empowered to honor God with my body. I am not my past—I've been redeemed and made new in Christ. I'm strong enough to say no when temptation comes. I choose purity because I know my worth. I'm led by the Spirit, not by my desires.I decree that every temptation sent to distract or detour me is dismantled in Jesus' name. I walk in holiness, purity, and self-discipline. My body belongs to God, not to the flesh. I won't be swayed by pressure, lust, or guilt. Abstinence is not a burden—it's my act of worship.

For the Woman Struggling with Lust and Perversion

"So I say, let the Holy Spirit guide your lives. Then you won't be doing what your sinful nature craves."- Galatians 5:16

Prayer

God,

I come to You with honesty , I've battled thoughts, desires, and patterns that I know don't reflect Your holiness. Whether it's from exposure, past experiences, or soul ties, I want to be free. I want a clean heart and a renewed mind. I no longer want to live in secrecy or shame. I renounce every spirit attached to lust, addiction, and perversion. Set me free, Lord. Teach me how to guard my eye gates, my ear gates, and my heart. In Jesus' name, Amen.

I Declare and Decree

I declare that I am no longer in bondage; I live knowing I am free through Christ. I am not ashamed of my struggle—I am redeemed and restored. I am made new, whole, and clean in God's eyes. I am not ruled by lust but led by God's love and truth. I walk in freedom, breaking cycles. I decree that every spirit of perversion, lust, and sexual addiction is broken off my life. I walk in purity, holiness, and integrity. Shame has no power over me. I will no longer be bound by secret battles. I am free, bold, and whole. I now have the mind of Christ and the heart of a worshipper.

For the Woman Struggling with Infertility

"I asked the Lord to give me this child, and he has granted my request."

- 1 Samuel 1:27

Prayer

Lord,

Month after month, I've carried quiet pain — watching others conceive while I wait. I've cried behind closed doors, battled disappointment, and wondered if something is wrong with me. But I still believe You are the Giver of life and the Author of miracles. I lay my womb, my hormones, my health, and my hope before You. Heal my heart in the waiting. Restore my body if needed. Strengthen my faith. Whether naturally, spiritually, or through adoption — I believe fruitfulness is my portion. In Jesus' name, Amen.

I Declare and Decree

I declare that I am not barren but full of promise. I am not forgotten—God sees me. I am not broken; I am beautifully created and divinely purposed. I remain hopeful, even in the waiting. I am surrounded by peace, not pressure.

I decree that infertility does not define me and God's promises still stand. My womb is healed, aligned, and blessed. Hope is rising in me again. Faith carries me through this journey, not fear or shame. No matter how God chooses, I will bear fruit and nurture life.

For the Woman Struggling with Drug and Alcohol Addiction

"So if the Son sets you free, you are truly free."- John 8:36

Prayer

Heavenly Father,

I'm tired of the cycle , tired of numbing pain with substances that only leave me emptier. I've used drugs or alcohol to escape, to forget, or to feel something. But the truth is, I want to be free. I want to feel whole again. I want to walk in purpose, not bondage. Lord, break the chains of addiction. Uproot the triggers, trauma, and lies that have led me here. Replace every craving with Your presence. Surround me with support and strength to stay clean, sober, and surrendered. I declare today that this is not how my story ends. In Jesus' name, Amen.

I Declare and Decree

I declare that I am not my addiction; I am a daughter of God. I am free from shame, guilt, and secrecy. I am being restored day by day —in my body, mind, and soul. I am stronger than every substance that once controlled me. I am no longer running; I am healing.

I decree that the spirit of addiction is broken off my life in Jesus' name. I will no longer seek comfort in chemicals but in Christ. I am walking in sobriety, peace, and clarity. I will be a testimony of recovery, not a prisoner of relapse. My body is a temple, and it will be honored and healed.

SECTION 4

Relationships, Roles, and Purpose

Chapter 8:

Called to Love and Lead

For the Woman Called to Love Deeply, Lead Boldly, and Live Unapologetically in Her God-Given Authority

For the Millennial Wife

"Her husband can trust her, and she will greatly enrich his life. She brings him good, not harm, all the days of her life."- Proverbs 31:11-12

Prayer

Lord,
Marriage in this generation comes with pressures and distractions — but I choose to center my covenant on You. Teach me how to love my husband with patience, grace, and wisdom. Show me how to lead in my home with humility, strength, and spiritual insight. Help me to balance purpose and partnership. I don't just want to be a wife in title — I want to be a helpmate in alignment. Build our foundation on You. In Jesus' name, Amen.

I Declare and Decree

I declare that I am graced to love, support, and partner in purpose. I am covered, valued, and led by the Spirit in my marriage. I am growing daily in wisdom, strength, and unity. I am not just a wife— I am a warrior, a nurturer, and a vessel of peace.

I decree that my marriage will reflect the heart of Christ. My role as a wife is protected, strengthened, and blessed. I will not lose myself in marriage, but I will grow and evolve through it. My marriage will bear fruit; emotionally, spiritually, and for generations to come.

For Wives of Faith

"A wise woman builds her home, but a foolish woman tears it down with her own hands."-Proverbs 14:1

Prayer

Father,
Thank You for entrusting me with the role of a faith-filled wife. When trials come, when we grow weary, remind me that You are in the center of it all. Strengthen my prayer life, deepen my intercession, and fill me with wisdom. Make me a safe place for my husband, a woman of joy, patience, and truth. Let my love reflect Your love — selfless, unshakable, and pure. In Jesus' name, Amen.

I Declare and Decree

I declare that I am a wife rooted in the Word and led by the Spirit. I am an intercessor, encourager, and spiritual pillar in my home. I am loved and honored, and I love with honor in return. I am equipped to walk beside my husband in faith and favor.

I decree that my home is a sanctuary of peace and spiritual alignment. My prayers will cover, protect, and bless my husband daily. God is the center of our covenant and the author of our legacy. I am rising in wisdom, favor, and divine strength as a wife of faith.

For the Woman Navigating Her Single Season

"For everything there is a season, a time for every activity under heaven." -Ecclesiastes 3:1

Prayer

Lord,
Singleness is not a punishment , but it feels like a sacred season. But some days are harder than others. I desire companionship, but I also desire to be whole before I enter covenant. Help me not to rush what You're preparing. Let this be the season where I become rooted in my identity, clarity, and calling. Teach me to steward this time well, grow closer to You, and trust that what's for me won't pass me by. In Jesus' name, Amen.

I Declare and Decree

I declare that I am whole, loved, and complete in Christ. I am not waiting to be chosen—I was already chosen by God. I am growing in purpose and peace in my single season. I am becoming the woman my future demands.

I decree that I will not idolize marriage, but honor my current season. I will not settle out of loneliness, but wait with wisdom. Singleness is not a delay; it's my season of divine preparation. My identity is not based on relationship status but rooted in Christ.

For the Single Mother Navigating Her Season

"Don't be afraid, for I am with you. Don't be discouraged, for I am your God. I will strengthen you and help you. I will hold you up with my victorious right hand." -Isaiah 41:10

Prayer

Lord,

Being a mother is a blessing — but doing it alone sometimes feels like a silent battle. There are days I feel overwhelmed, unseen, and unsure of how to carry it all. But You see me. You've graced me for this assignment. Remind me that I am not raising these children by myself — You are parenting with me. Fill every gap. Strengthen me when I'm weary. Provide when the needs feel greater than the resources. Heal every part of me that longs for companionship, but help me not to settle in desperation. Let this single season be filled with strength, strategy, peace, and purpose. In Jesus' name, Amen.

I Declare and Decree

I declare that I am not alone; I am partnered with the Holy Spirit in motherhood. I am strong, even on the days I feel stretched. I am raising my children in love, faith, and wisdom. I am enough, even when I feel inadequate. I am not forgotten—this season has purpose and divine preparation.

I decree that my children are covered, protected, and provided for. I will raise them from a place of faith, not fear. My single season is not a punishment but a platform, and I am worthy of love again. God is sending supernatural strength, community, and provision. Joy, balance, and breakthrough belong to me and my household.

Chapter 9:

Called to Build and Breakthrough

For the Woman Called to Build What's Never Been Done and Break Through What Tried to Break Her

For the Kingdom Business Woman / Business Woman

"Remember the Lord your God. He is the one who gives you power to be successful, in order to fulfill the covenant he confirmed to your ancestors with an oath." -Deuteronomy 8:18

Prayer

Heavenly Father,

You've entrusted me with vision, creativity, and the grace to build. I surrender every idea, strategy, and assignment to You. Help me not to chase success, but to seek significance. Let my business be rooted in Kingdom principles, integrity, excellence, impact. Show me how to lead without burnout, steward finances wisely, and trust You in every launch, pivot, and process. In Jesus' name, Amen.

I Declare and Decree

I declare that I am a visionary, called to lead and create. I am not just building a business—I'm building a legacy. I am favored, fruitful, and focused. I am called to create wealth that advances the Kingdom.I decree that my business will prosper and impact lives. Divine connections and resources are locating me. No weapon formed against my business will prosper. I lead with faith, wisdom, and strategy straight from Heaven.

For the Woman Who Thinks "It's Too Late"

"The LORD says, 'I will give you back what you lost to the swarming locusts, the hopping locusts, the stripping locusts, and the cutting locusts. It was I who sent this great destroying army against you."

-Joel 2:25

Prayer

God,

There are times I've believed the lie that it's too late for me. That I've missed my chance, that my dreams are expired. But I'm reminded that You are the Redeemer of time. What I thought was delay was actually development. Breathe life back into the places I gave up on. Revive the passion, the dream, and the boldness to try again. Show me that age, mistakes, or time passed can never cancel purpose. In Jesus' name, Amen.

I Declare and Decree

I declare that I am right on time for God's perfect will. I am not behind—I am being positioned. I am stepping into a new season with boldness and faith. I am still becoming who God called me to be. I decree that it is not too late; my life is in alignment with God's divine timing. Delayed and dead dreams are being resurrected. I will not be bound by the timeline of man but led by the timing of God. My best years are not behind me, they're unfolding now.

For the Woman Struggling with Her Finances

"And this same God who takes care of me will supply all your needs from his glorious riches, which have been given to us in Christ Jesus."
-Philippians 4:19

Prayer

Lord,
You see my heart and You see my bank account. You know the anxiety I feel when bills are due, when there's more need than money, and when I wonder how it will all work out. I want to trust You as my Provider, not just with my salvation , but with my finances. Help me break every cycle of lack, fear, overspending, and poor stewardship. Teach me to manage what You've given me with wisdom, strategy, and gratitude. I declare that this is not my forever — breakthrough is on the way. In Jesus' name, Amen.

I Declare and Decree

I declare that I am not broke; I am blessed, highly favored, and being built for more. I am a steward, not just a spender. I am wise with my finances and faithful with my increase. I trust God to be my source—not the paycheck, the job, or the world. I am breaking free from financial fear and walking in provision. I am a lender, not a borrower. I decree that financial lack and fear are broken off me and my household. Supernatural provision, ideas, and resources are locating me now. I will owe no one anything but love (Romans 13:8). I have more than enough to live, to give, and to build. Generational poverty ends with me today, and abundance begins now.

For the Woman Struggling in Corporate/ Professional Settings

"Whenever the king consulted them in any matter requiring wisdom and balanced judgment, he found them ten times more capable than any of the magicians and enchanters in his entire kingdom."

- Daniel 1:20

Prayer

Lord,

You've placed me in this corporate/ Professional space , but there are days I feel like I don't belong. The pressure to perform, the weight of expectations, and the subtle battles I face behind the scenes sometimes leave me tired and second-guessing. But I believe You've called me to be a light in this space and not to blend in, but to bring Kingdom wherever I go.

Help me to lead with integrity, show up with confidence, and walk in purpose even in rooms that weren't built for me. Cover me when I feel overlooked, empower me when I feel outnumbered, and remind me that my work is worship. You are my true boss, my ultimate source, and my daily strength. In Jesus' name, Amen.

I Declare and Decree

I declare that I'm not just working for a paycheck, I'm walking in divine placement. I am strong, wise, and capable, even when I feel stretched. I'm not shrinking to fit into spaces; I'm rising to transform them. I am led by the Spirit, even in boardrooms. I am graced for this assignment and will not lose myself in it. I decree that I will not allow pressure to steal my peace or identity. I am favored, respected, and recognized, even when unseen by man. God is opening doors, providing strategy, and shifting atmospheres through me. My gifts are making room for me and placing me before great men (Proverbs 18:16). I will not just survive this job—I will thrive, grow, and influence.

For the Woman Struggling in Ministry

"So let's not get tired of doing what is good. At just the right time we will reap a harvest of blessing if we don't give up."-Galatians 6:9

Prayer

Lord,

You called me and I said yes. But if I'm honest, ministry has stretched me, tested me, and at times worn me down. There are moments I've questioned if I'm really equipped... if anyone sees what I pour... or if what I do even matters. But I know You didn't bring me this far to leave me here.

Remind me why I said yes. Restore the joy of serving You. Help me not to carry the weight of ministry without remaining in the presence of the One who sent me. Teach me to rest, to reset, and to refill so I'm not ministering from an empty place. Anoint me again. Strengthen me again. Breathe fresh wind into my assignment. In Jesus' name, Amen.

I Declare and Decree

I declare that I am called, chosen, equipped, and anointed, even on hard days. I am not performing for people, but positioned by God. I am not forgotten or overlooked—Heaven sees every seed I sow. I am doing holy work, and my obedience matters. I am not burned out; I am being refreshed and reignited. I decree that discouragement, weariness, and isolation are breaking off me now. I serve from a place of overflow, not depletion. Divine strength, strategy, and support are locating me. I am planted, protected, and powerfully equipped for ministry.

A Final Word of Encouragement

Im so proud of you, you didn't just finish declaring and decreeing , you activated destiny. You broke patterns. You silenced lies. You spoke life. Whether you cried, warred, worshipped, or whispered your way through these pages, know this: you showed up for your healing and Heaven showed up for you.

Freedom doesn't always look loud. Sometimes it's quiet and daily.
But it's real.
And it belongs to you.

Keep declaring. Keep praying. Keep growing.
God is not finished with you yet ! and you're not going back to what He already delivered you from.
This is your new beginning.

"Being confident of this, that He who began a good work in you will carry it on to completion..." — Philippians 1:6

What's Next?

- **Revisit** this book as needed. Healing is a journey, not a one-time event.

- **Share** your favorite declarations with other women. Be the light for someone else.

- **Journal** your progress. Re-read your growth. Celebrate your spiritual wins.

- **Pray boldly.** Heaven hears you and responds to faith.

- **Join community.** You don't have to walk this alone.

Tools for the Journey

Gratitude Prayer

Heavenly Father,

Thank You for walking with me through this journey. Thank You for every broken chain, every stronghold dismantled, every lie silenced, and every truth revealed. Thank You for being my constant and refuge —my healer, my deliverer, my guide, and my strength. You were present through every tear, every revelation, and every declaration I made in faith.

Today, I boldly come out of agreement with fear, shame, guilt, unworthiness, silence, bondage, and every generational curse that tried to define me. I come out of agreement with every label that wasn't spoken by You. And I come fully into agreement with Your Word, Your truth, Your promises, and Your divine will for my life.

Lord, I ask that You seal every page I've read and every declaration I've spoken with Your Spirit. Let this not just be an emotional moment, but a spiritual *marking* — a true *activation* of my identity, healing, and purpose. Let the words I've prayed echo in the atmosphere and shift everything in my life that is not aligned with Heaven.

From this day forward, I will walk in freedom. I will declare Your truth. I will live with intention.
And I will never be the same.

In the mighty name of Jesus,
Amen.

NOTES

NOTES

NOTES

NOTES

NOTES

Scripture Reference

Psalm 139:14 – "Thank you for making me so wonderfully complex! Your workmanship is marvelous—how well I know it."

Colossians 2:10 – "So you also are complete through your union with Christ, who is the head over every ruler and authority."

Romans 8:38–39 – "Nothing can separate us from the love of God…"

Jeremiah 31:3 – "I have loved you with an everlasting love…"

2 Corinthians 3:5–6 – "Our qualification comes from God…"

Philippians 4:13 – "I can do all things through Christ who gives me strength."

Revelation 3:8 – "I have opened a door for you that no one can close."

Song of Songs 4:7 – "You are altogether beautiful, my darling, beautiful in every way."

Genesis 1:27 – "So God created human beings in His own image…"

2 Corinthians 10:4–5 – "We use God's mighty weapons…to knock down strongholds…"

Galatians 6:2 – "Share each other's burdens, and in this way obey the law of Christ."

2 Corinthians 12:9 – "My grace is sufficient for you, for my power is made perfect in weakness."

Psalm 34:18 – "The Lord is close to the brokenhearted…"

Exodus 20:5–6 – "I lay the sins of the parents upon their children... But I lavish unfailing love..."

Isaiah 61:1 – "He has sent me to comfort the brokenhearted..."

Psalm 147:3 – "He heals the brokenhearted and binds up their wounds."

Psalm 27:10 – "Even if my father and mother abandon me, the Lord will hold me close."

Matthew 5:4 – "God blesses those who mourn, for they will be comforted."

Psalm 34:18 (again) – "The Lord is close to the brokenhearted..."

Isaiah 66:13 – "I will comfort you there as a mother comforts her child."

Revelation 21:4 – "He will wipe every tear from their eyes..."

Colossians 3:13 – "Forgive anyone who offends you. Remember, the Lord forgave you..."

1 John 1:9 – "If we confess our sins, He is faithful...to forgive us..."

Romans 8:1 – "There is now no condemnation for those who are in Christ Jesus."

Isaiah 43:18–19 – "Forget the former things... I am doing

Proverbs 3:5-6 – "Trust in the Lord with all your heart; do not depend on your own understanding. Seek his will in all you do, and he will show you which path to take."

James 4:7 – "So humble yourselves before God. Resist the devil, and he will flee from you."

Isaiah 26:3 – "You will keep in perfect peace all who trust in you, all whose thoughts are fixed on you!"

Jeremiah 29:11 – "For I know the plans I have for you," says the Lord. "They are plans for good and not for disaster, to give you a future and a hope."

1 Corinthians 6:19-20 – "Don't you realize that your body is the temple of the Holy Spirit, who lives in you and was given to you by God? You do not belong to yourself, for God bought you with a high price. So you must honor God with your body."

Galatians 5:16 – "So I say, let the Holy Spirit guide your lives. Then you won't be doing what your sinful nature craves."

1 Samuel 1:27 – "I asked the Lord to give me this child, and he has granted my request."

John 8:36 – "So if the Son sets you free, you are truly free."

Proverbs 31:11-12 – "Her husband can trust her, and she will greatly enrich his life. She brings him good, not harm, all the days of her life."

Proverbs 14:1 – "A wise woman builds her home, but a foolish woman tears it down with her own hands."

Ecclesiastes 3:1 – "For everything there is a season, a time for every activity under heaven."

Isaiah 41:10 – "Don't be afraid, for I am with you. Don't be discouraged, for I am your God. I will strengthen you and help you. I will hold you up with my victorious right hand."

Deuteronomy 8:18 – "Remember the Lord your God. He is the one who gives you power to be successful, in order to fulfill the covenant he confirmed to your ancestors with an oath."

Joel 2:25 – "The LORD says, 'I will give you back what you lost to the swarming locusts, the hopping locusts, the stripping locusts, and the cutting locusts. It was I who sent this great destroying army against you.'"

Philippians 4:19 – "And this same God who takes care of me will supply all your needs from his glorious riches, which have been given to us in Christ Jesus."

Daniel 1:20 – "Whenever the king consulted them in any matter requiring wisdom and balanced judgment, he found them ten times more capable than any of the magicians and enchanters in his entire kingdom."

Romans 13:8 – "Owe no one anything, except to love each other."

Galatians 6:9 – "So let's not get tired of doing what is good. At just the right time we will reap a harvest of blessing if we don't give up."

28-Day Declaration Challenge Tracker

This 28-day challenge was created to help you *intentionally* speak life over yourself every single day. As believers, we are reminded in Proverbs 18:21 that *"life and death are in the power of the tongue"*. what we speak carries weight in the spiritual realm. Declaring God's Word daily allows us to align our thoughts, actions, and atmosphere with His truth, even when our feelings or circumstances try to convince us otherwise.

This tracker is your tool of accountability and spiritual discipline. Each day, take a few moments to **boldly declare God's promises** over your life. Speak them aloud with faith, confidence, and expectation, knowing that His Word does not return void (Isaiah 55:11).

Use the space provided to:

1. Check off the day once completed

2. Write down the declarations you spoke

3. Record any scriptures that stood out to you or resonated with your current season

4. Reflect briefly on how those words made you feel or what you sensed God saying to you

Whether you're declaring healing, restoration, peace, identity, provision, or purpose, this tracker is meant to help you remain *rooted in truth and consistent in faith*.

WEEK 1

	MON	TUE	WED	THU	FRI	SUT	SUN
	○	○	○	○	○	○	○
	○	○	○	○	○	○	○
	○	○	○	○	○	○	○
	○	○	○	○	○	○	○
	○	○	○	○	○	○	○

WEEK 2

	MON	TUE	WED	THU	FRI	SUT	SUN
	○	○	○	○	○	○	○
	○	○	○	○	○	○	○
	○	○	○	○	○	○	○
	○	○	○	○	○	○	○
	○	○	○	○	○	○	○

WEEK 3

	MON	TUE	WED	THU	FRI	SUT	SUN
	○	○	○	○	○	○	○
	○	○	○	○	○	○	○
	○	○	○	○	○	○	○
	○	○	○	○	○	○	○
	○	○	○	○	○	○	○

WEEK 4

	MON	TUE	WED	THU	FRI	SUT	SUN
	○	○	○	○	○	○	○
	○	○	○	○	○	○	○
	○	○	○	○	○	○	○
	○	○	○	○	○	○	○
	○	○	○	○	○	○	○

Heart Check Questions For The Soul

Identity & Healing

1. How have past wounds or hurts shaped your view of yourself, and how can you begin to see yourself through God's eyes as healed and whole?

2. What areas in your life do you need to intentionally release to God for forgiveness and restoration?

Freedom & Grace

1. In what ways do you feel spiritually or emotionally imprisoned, and how can you step into the freedom that God promises?

2. How does embracing grace change the way you approach your daily struggles or mistakes?

God's Presence & Assurance

1. When have you most deeply felt God's presence in your life? How can you cultivate more awareness of His nearness?

2. How do God's promises encourage you when you face uncertainty or fear?

Strength & Resilience

1. What challenges are you currently facing that require you to stand firm in faith and declare God's truth over your situation?

2. How can decreeing God's Word empower you to overcome doubt and build resilience?

Purpose & Calling

1. What do you believe God is calling you to step into right now, and how can prayer support you in that journey?

2. How does declaring God's truth help align your thoughts and actions with His purpose for your life?

How To Write Your Own Decree

Activate Your Voice. Declare God's Word. Shift the Atmosphere.

In this section, I want you to practice writing your own decree.One that speaks directly to where you are and what you're believing God for. Use the truth of His Word as your foundation, and write with boldness, faith, and authority. This is your moment to activate your voice and declare what Heaven says about you.

1. Start with God's Word (Scripture)

- Find a scripture that speaks directly to the area you want to decree over (healing, identity, fear, provision, purpose, etc.)

- Example: *"I am fearfully and wonderfully made"* – *Psalm 139:14*

Prompt:
What verse is speaking to your heart today? Write it below.

2. Identify the Truth You Want to Stand On

Ask: *What does God say about this situation?*
You're not begging — you're **agreeing** with what's already written in Heaven.

Prompt:
Write 1–2 truths you believe God is speaking over your life right now.

3. Use Bold, Present-Tense Language

Your decree should sound like this:

- **"I am..."**

- **"I walk in..."**

- **"I declare..."**

- **"I break off..."**

- **"I release..."**
  Avoid "I will" or "I hope" — decree from a place of **faith now.**

Decree Template:

"I decree that [insert your faith statement], according to [insert scripture reference]."

4. Speak with Authority

Say it aloud. Over your life, your home, your family.
Your words partner with Heaven and carry creative power (Proverbs 18:21).

Example Decrees:

- *"I decree that I am whole and healed — body, soul, and spirit — according to Isaiah 53:5."*

- *"I decree that I lack nothing because the Lord is my Shepherd (Psalm 23:1)."*

5. Write Your Own Decree

Use this space to write your personal decree:

"I decree that…"

_____

_____

_____

_____

_____

_____

_____

_____

_____

_____

_____

_____

6. Declare It Daily

A decree becomes powerful when spoken consistently.
Challenge: Speak your decree aloud every day for 7 days.
Watch what shifts.

The Lie & The Truth

We've all believed lies ! Some whispered by our past, some shouted by our insecurities, and others subtly planted by the enemy. But as daughters of the Most High, we are called to tear down every lie that exalts itself against the knowledge of God (2 Corinthians 10:5).

In this activity, take a moment to identify the lie, then replace it with God's truth from Scripture.

Instructions:

1. Think of a lie you've believed about yourself, your identity, your worth, or your future.

2. Find and write a truth from Scripture that breaks that lie.

3. Speak the truth aloud as a declaration over your life.

Example :

The Lie	The Truth (Scripture)
I'm not enough	I am God's workmanship – Ephesians 2:10
I'll always be broken	By His wounds, I am healed – Isaiah 53:5
God won't come through	God is faithful to all His promises – Psalm 145:13

Your Turn:

The Lie	The Truth (Scripture)

Keep this page close. Revisit it. Add to it. Speak truth every time the lie tries to return. The Word of God is your sword.

Want to Go Deeper?

Discover the Story Behind the Strength.

If this devotional stirred something in your spirit, then *Rise & Radiate: A Transformative Journey of Faith and Resilience* is your next step. In this raw and empowering book, Ashlyn shares her personal journey through pain, healing, identity, and purpose. It's not just a memoir, it's a roadmap for every woman who's ever wrestled with self-worth, generational cycles, emotional wounds, and the call to rise despite it all.

Whether you're in a season of rebuilding, rediscovery, or rising again, this book was written with *you* in mind. Your healing matters. Your voice matters. Your purpose is waiting.

Grab your copy today and let your healing journey begin.
Visit: www.ashlynmeraz.com

Stay Connected

■ Website
Explore resources, devotionals, and coaching opportunities: www.ashlynmeraz.com

🎙 Listen In
Tune into the *Purely You Podcast* for real conversations, biblical encouragement, and wisdom for the woman becoming.
Available on Apple Podcasts, Spotify & more

Let's Connect on Instagram
Follow me @ashlynmareigh and @purelyyoupodcast for daily encouragement, behind-the-scenes, and live chats.

📧 Join the Email List
Be the first to know about upcoming books, virtual studies, prayer challenges, and coaching programs.
Sign up at www.ashlynmeraz.com

Need Coaching or Prayer?
If you're ready to go deeper, rise stronger, and walk boldly in who God called you to be, I invite you to explore 1:1 Christian life coaching with me.
Let's walk it out together: www.ashlynmeraz.com/coaching

AUTHOR

Ashlyn Meraz is a life coach, entrepreneur, speaker, and author passionate about helping women step into their God-given purpose. With a heart rooted in faith, resilience, and transformation, she empowers women to heal, grow, and thrive—spiritually and personally—through life's many seasons.

Born and raised in Bradenton, Florida, Ashlyn discovered *strength and creative* expression through faith, art, and sports from an early age. Her journey of overcoming adversity has deeply shaped her calling to inspire and equip others through coaching, podcasting, and purpose-driven content creation.

As the host of the *Purely You Podcast* and founder of *Rise & Radiate Coaching*, Ashlyn is committed to helping women deepen their faith, embrace their identity, and live boldly. Whether through writing, coaching, or speaking, her mission is to encourage, uplift, and ignite lasting transformation.

To learn more visit **www.ashlynmeraz.com**

www.ingramcontent.com/pod-product-compliance
Lightning Source LLC
Chambersburg PA
CBHW031250120626
46545CB00007B/2738